Wheels

written by Jacquie Kilkenny

What is a Wheel?

A wheel is round like a circle.

circle

Wheels help us to move things from place to place.

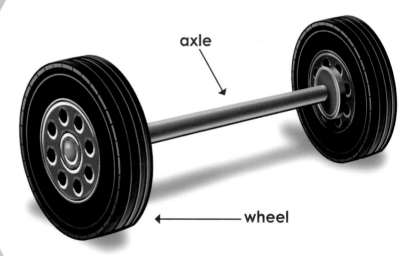

axle

wheel

To make a wheel move,
we have to push or pull it along.

4

Wheels roll round and round when they move.

Wheels Help Us

Wheels help us to push or to pull things.

If you had a very heavy box
and you had to push it along the ground,
you could not do it.

If the box was in a *wheelbarrow*,
or even on a *skateboard*,
the wheels would help you to move it.

Where We Find Wheels

When we think of wheels,
we often think of *cars* and *bicycles*.
Cars, bicycles and *motorbikes*
all need wheels to move.
Trains, buses, tractors and *aeroplanes*
also need wheels to move.

We could not ride a *scooter* or a skateboard if they did not have wheels.

You could not push a baby in a *pram* if the pram did not have wheels.

Wheels are all around us.

A *fairground* has lots of wheels.
Can you see them?

A *big wheel* is an enormous wheel.

A *roundabout* in a *playground* is also a large wheel.
When children run and push the roundabout,
they make it spin round and round.

Some wheels are big and some are small.
There are lots of wheels that we can't see.

Inside a *car engine* there are wheels.
These wheels help the engine to move the car.

Inside a *watch* there are tiny wheels.
These wheels help the watch to go.

Wheels Are Everywhere

- Wheels help us to get from place to place.
- Wheels help us to push and pull things.
- Wheels help to make things work.
- Wheels help us to have fun.

Wheels are everywhere.

Look around!

Can you see a wheel?

What would it be like if:
- your *toys* did not have wheels?
- your bike did not have wheels?

Picture Glossary

aeroplanes

car engine

roundabout

trains

bicycles

fairground

scooter

watch

big wheel

motorbikes

skateboard

wheelbarrow

buses

playground

toys

cars

pram

tractors